Praying Our Way
Through Life

M. Basilea Schlink

Evangelical Sisterhood of Mary
Darmstadt-Eberstadt, Germany

© Evangelical Sisterhood of Mary, 1991

ISBN 3-87209-636-2

Original title: *Mein Beten*
First German edition 1969
First English edition 1970
This edition 1991, revised English translation

Unless otherwise stated, all Bible quotations are taken from
the Revised Standard Version of the Bible, copyrighted 1946,
1952, 1971 and 1973, and used by permission.
Bible quotations identified GNB are taken from the Good
News Bible — Old Testament: Copyright © American Bible
Society 1976, New Testament: Copyright © American Bible
Society 1966, 1971, 1976, and used by permission.

Branch address for U.S.A.:

Evangelical Sisterhood of Mary
9849 North 40th Street
Phoenix, Arizona 85028

Printed in the United States of America

Contents

Introduction

Time and again we read in the Bible the call to prayer. When Scripture says "Pray!", it does not mean that we should hastily snatch a bit of time for prayer now and then, perhaps in the morning or evening. Important though it is to set a regular time for communing with the Lord or for intercession, all this is not enough. As the beloved of the Lord and as His chosen ones, we are destined for something far greater, far more wonderful! He has called us to a whole life of prayer, a life of constant communion with Him. Prayer has many varied modes of expression, and only if these different forms are manifest in our lives, are we truly leading a life of prayer.

First of all, we are familiar with the prayer of supplication when we come as a child before the heavenly Father with our personal requests. Then there is the prayer of faith, which often involves wrestling in prayer in accordance with Jesus' words, "This kind never comes out except by prayer and fasting" (Matthew 17:21). The prayer of faith is applied especially in intercession. Another form of prayer is thanksgiving, which is akin to praise and worship. The Lord also wants to grant us the prayer of the heart, unceasing prayer, during which the soul is in constant communion with God. If we live in this state of prayer, we will naturally be moved to practise the other forms of prayer as well. It is the Spirit of God who prompts us to turn to God and then also to wrestle in prayer for others and to offer up praise and worship. This is the kind of prayer life God wants us to have. He delights in showing us goodness and, well knowing that nothing will bring such blessing in our life as prayer, He desires to transform it into a life of prayer.

As a man of God once expressed it, "Prayer is the greatest power on earth. It can move the hand of Him who rules the world!" Yes, prayer is a matchless opportunity. For through prayer we can change everything: people, things, problems and circumstances. Prayer has infinite power. And for this reason Satan tries everything to prevent us from praying. He knows that we are not a real danger to him when we work and accomplish a great deal — even if it is for the Kingdom of God. But when we pray much, we invade Satan's dominion and rob him of his captives. There is nothing Satan dreads so much as our prayers.

Praying When Problems and Troubles Arise

Difficulties arising in our life, in our job or family can be a warning sign from God. He may have a purpose in allowing them to come. Perhaps He wants to use them to train us or chasten us, because our life needs to be changed — either in a specific area or in general. In such cases we cannot simply pray away the difficulties. We have to accept them as the chisel of God and allow Him to shape us.

In the history of our Sisterhood I have often seen how God has let difficulties pile up in order to alert us to something that had displeased Him. Whenever we came into such situations, our first prayer was: "Lord, enlighten us by Your Holy Spirit of truth. Show us what is grieving You. Show us why You are placing so many problems and troubles in our way and why You have to chasten us." Such prayers for the Spirit of truth have the greatest promise of being answered. He always showed us our "sore spot" very clearly. Then, claiming the redeeming power of the sacrifice of Jesus, we fought an intensive battle of prayer against it. When God had achieved His objective with us and we repented of the sins and failures He showed us and turned over a new leaf, the difficulties disappeared by themselves after a while. God removed them, because He had attained His purpose.

When we come into situations where we cannot simply pray away the difficulties, we are not only to humble ourselves beneath His powerful hand, submitting to chastening for our improvement. We should also appeal to our heavenly Father. As His children, we should beg

Him to display His power and to remove the difficulties.

This is true especially when the difficulties are hindering His cause and the advance of the Kingdom of God. In such situations the Lord has shown me that in faith I should praise God for who He is and for the greatness of His power and the strength of His arm. He challenged me to declare that nothing is impossible for Him, that mountains have to melt like wax before Him, and that He can resolve difficulties with a single word.

In the many difficulties we have faced in the ministries of our Sisterhood, we have fought such battles of faith over and over again together. We have spent many hours in prayer, declaring to the Lord in word or song the greatness of His power and glory and love. In His love He always wants to help His children and has a solution to their problems. I cannot count the times when the Lord has answered such prayers of faith and we have received the necessary help, even if we had to wait a long time. Indeed, the greater the difficulties, the more wonderful the Lord has proved Himself to be when we have persevered with our prayers of faith and praises of His omnipotence.

The Lord also leads us into difficulties to teach us not to focus on the visible things, however serious the problems may be. Instead of relying on our own resources, we are to rely on Him alone — the almighty, powerful Lord, the caring

Father. Through such prayers of faith He wants to give us a special blessing in the midst of difficulties. He wants to give us an experience of the living God that we might not have otherwise.

Impossibilities and hopeless situations are also an opportunity to glorify the Lord before the visible and invisible world, for nothing is so honouring to Him as when we pray in faith and proclaim His greatness. And so I can only be thankful for the many difficulties which God has placed in my way and in the way of our Sisterhood. They showed us our sore spots; they led us into repentance and a deeper experience of the saving, transforming power of Jesus' blood. They taught us to have faith in His power and help, which we then witnessed in answer to prayer. They filled our hearts anew with the adoration of our Lord. They spurred us on to testify to our God and Father, and now many others are inspired to give God glory.

Praying in Dark Days of Suffering

All of us are acquainted with dark days of suffering. Perhaps we have been greatly disappointed. Perhaps a loved one has been taken from us. Perhaps we are sick or lonely. In over sixty years of walking with Jesus I have found that one thing is of supreme importance: not to allow suffering to absorb us, nor to let it so weigh us down that we become more or less paralyzed in prayer. The Holy Spirit has shown me how essential it is for us to take our refuge in prayer if we want to gain the victory in suffering. Now is the very moment to tell Jesus that we trust Him and that we believe He can deal with our suffering.

I have discovered how vital it is to believe that Jesus is greater than my suffering. That is, He has ways of dealing with it. In His love He wants to help us at all costs. He wants to pour balm on our comfortless, wounded hearts. We need to believe that God will grant us comfort in dark days of suffering. Anyone who prays for this, trusting that God will answer his prayer, will experience it.

Jesus stands by everyone who bears sorrow. He is there as the source of eternal, divine life. He lets a measure of His divine life, which is peace and heavenly joy, flow into us. Then everything is transformed. Our comfortless hearts are filled with comfort, peace and heavenly joy.

In the words of a German hymn, "In You we have joy amid sorrow and grief, O sweet Lord Jesus Christ!" That is a truth to which I can bear witness. In periods of loneliness and sorrow I have known the love of Jesus Christ, which brings the fullness of joy into our hearts. In physical sickness and pain, in spiritual suffering and inner conflict I have discovered that the presence of Jesus is triumphant. It was especially in such times that I was led into a deeper fellowship with Him. When loved ones were taken from me, I found that Jesus' comfort was greater than all the grief in my heart.

Many others have had the same experience in their life of discipleship and can join me in testifying to it. Looking back, they would not have missed these dark days of suffering for anything because of the blessing they discovered in prayer. So in dark days of suffering, have faith and pray, "I commit my ways to the Lord. He will lead me aright." Then you, too, will experience that His ways are perfect and that He really does comfort you.

Praying When No Answer Seems to Come

Whenever my prayers have remained unanswered, the Lord has first led me to ask whether there were prayer hindrances. He has often shown me that there was a sin standing in the way, a sin of which I had not been so conscious — for example, a spirit of criticism or bitterness. That is why the Lord was not listening. "Behold, the Lord's hand is not shortened, that it cannot save, or his ear dull, that it cannot hear; but your iniquities have made a separation between you and your God, and your sins have hid his face from you so that he does not hear" (Isaiah 59:1,2).

Holy Scripture gives many examples of sin as an obstacle to prayer: unwillingness to forgive (Matthew 6:15), anger, quarrelling (1 Timothy 2:8), lack of reconciliation (Matthew 5:23,24), all sensuality and gratification of our passions (1 Peter 4:7; James 4:3), involvement with the occult (Deuteronomy 18:10-12), disobedience (John 9:31), reluctance to confess our sins before one another (James 5:16), greed, for "give, and it will be given to you; good measure, pressed down, shaken together, running over . . ." (Luke 6:38).

When it comes to prayer, we need to remember that "the eyes of the Lord are toward the righteous, and his ears toward their cry" (Psalm 34:15; cf. James 5:16). The Word of God is valid. Often when it has seemed as though God were not answering our prayers, He has shown us that He could not, because we were not counted among the "righteous".

We were not righteous before God, because our hearts were not filled with repentance. Only those who humbly admit their daily failures before God and man are righteous in His sight. Their sin is cancelled by the blood of the Lamb.

Our sinful nature, taken as a whole, does not constitute an obstacle to prayer. If that were so, God could never answer any prayers. Rather, a prayer obstacle is an unconfessed sin, from which we do not want to part. We need to come to the cross with a contrite heart and confess our guilt before others, because we are sorry. We need to remove that which grieves God or our fellow-men by turning over a new leaf. Then God can be gracious to us again and answer our prayers. Time and again this has been our experience as a Sisterhood. For instance, if two Sisters had a disagreement and then made up, "God's ears were opened again" and our prayers were answered. In the book *Realities — The Miracles of God Experienced Today* (American edition: *Realities of Faith*) there are several testimonies about this.

However, there can be another reason behind unanswered prayers. God does not answer the prayer of a defiant heart. The servant with only one talent said that God was a "hard man" (Matthew 25:24). Only childlike souls have access to God's heart. They trust and believe that He is a Father and wants to help them. They believe that He always has a solution prepared and has only good intentions in mind.

We will experience God in our prayer life just as we think of Him. If we think and say, "He is a hard master", we will experience harshness — just like the servant who was thrown into the outer darkness. Or consider the people of Israel. In the wilderness they did not believe that God had good intentions. On the contrary, they thought that God wanted them to perish in the wilderness. As a result they really did fail to reach the promised land. Because of their distrustful attitude towards God, that generation perished in the wilderness. Joshua and Caleb, who trusted God, were the only ones to survive the forty years of wandering and were permitted to enter Canaan. Whenever defiance and rebellion against God have found room in our hearts, a wall is erected so that the good things which God wants to give us cannot reach us. And then our prayers remain unanswered.

The first step to having our prayers answered is a searching of our consciences, so that the Lord can show us the obstacles to prayer mentioned in the Scriptures. The next step is to ask for repentance and to make a new start. The prerequisite for answered prayer is having a right relationship with God — without any hidden defiance — and also with our fellow-men.

Apart from sinful attitudes and actions, there can be yet another reason why our prayers are not answered — at least for a while. God may be training us. In this case the fact that our prayers are not answered should challenge us to persist in prayer. God is waiting for more prayer and more faith on our part. During the acquisition of our land of Canaan, which we needed for our ministry, we stumbled upon one difficulty after another. It seemed as though God were not answering our prayers. Still, it was His plan to give us Canaan and to honour all our prayers.

But a condition was attached — we had to persevere in prayer. While the fulfilment of our prayers was being delayed, we were being inwardly prepared to lead our life at Canaan in His spirit. Waiting for the fulfilment of our prayers was a school of preparation. Waiting teaches us patience. It teaches us to keep on believing. It makes us humble. It purifies us and transforms us.

Every time we persevere in prayer because an answer is not immediately forthcoming, we need to know whether our request is according to God's will. Holy Scripture shows us that this is a prerequisite, especially when praying for others. Or sometimes we have received a definite promise, which is to be claimed in persevering prayer. We can count on this prayer being answered, even if it seems humanly impossible.

The deepest solution to all unanswered prayer, in my experience, lies in the unity of the will with God. If we pray all our prayers in the attitude, "Not my will, but Yours be done", then we know that there are actually no unanswered prayers. God hears them all. We just have to leave it to Him as to how and when He will answer them. He alone knows what is best for us and for His kingdom. Because God is love, He will always lead us the best way. If we know this, we will no longer be surprised if He answers our prayers in a different manner or at a different time than we expect.

Praying in Times of Spiritual Dryness

We all know times when we have no desire to pray. It seems to us as though our prayers bounce back from the walls and do not rise to God. Time and again we pass through such periods. Our soul is so arid and dried out that it seems as though the Holy Spirit has forsaken us.

If there is no prayer obstacle to prevent our prayers from rising to God, He must be leading us purposely through such dry periods. A plan of God is behind it. God's plans are always wonderful. They always lead to a marvellous goal and ultimately to glory. Now everything depends upon our making use of this time and being victorious in it. God has taught me that such times do not have to be empty and unfruitful but can yield a special blessing.

If we can hardly formulate a single thought of our own in prayer, because everything seems to be dead in us, then we can still engage in intercession by proclaiming the victorious name of Jesus over the various prayer requests or by praying hymns or litanies of victory.

This prayer in inner night holds special blessing and will be heard. It is a prayer without the spiritual enjoyment we have when we can sense the Spirit driving us to prayer. Praying at such times costs us something. We really have to make an effort. For this reason it is precious to the Lord. Special fruit will come from these prayers, even though we may think they are not reaching God at all.

But I have also discovered that there is a way of making our prayers come alive in such times of aridity — through thanksgiving. This is the opportunity God gives us. I have a thanksgiving booklet, and each evening I write down everything I have to thank God for. But I also have another booklet in which I keep a record of the main points of thanksgiving for each year. I take up these points one by one, thank God for them, or sing Him a song of thanksgiving. Then these prayers help me to reach the point where I am able to thank Him even for the times of spiritual darkness. Now I begin to praise and thank Him for the new life born in such times of night and drought. These periods cleanse my soul from all the dross, from unspiritual love and human enthusiasm for prayer. New spiritual life is born out of the spiritual death the soul has to suffer. Every time I praise Him for this, I am strengthened and comforted, and prayer comes more easily to me.

During one such time I wrote the song:

> I sing, I sing, God adoring,
> My praise to heaven upsoaring.
> May my psalmody
> Give pleasure to Thee.

Verse after verse followed as I sang in praise of everything that was difficult for me — trials and temptations, pathways through the night —

and the blessing such times brought me; the joy of being able to fulfil God's will in spiritual night.

The paralyzing sense of death withdrew. My heart was comforted by saying Yes to the will of God and to His ways — even when they led through aridity and darkness.

I'll sing of God's will in sadness,
Of how obeying brings gladness.
When we do His will,
All sorrow is stilled.

I sing, God's heart is all loving;
He takes no pleasure in chastening.
Because I'm His child,
His discipline's mild.

I praise Thy ruling and guiding,
The way Thou chosest to lead me.
E'en paths through the night
With blessings were bright.

I'll sing in pain and in sorrow,
In grief and fear of the morrow.
Thy praise shall remain
My constant refrain.

I'll sing of God's grace and mercy,
The aid His love ever brings me.
He helps me indeed
In sadness and need.

I'll sing, my grief will be ended,
One day by gladness transcended

In heaven above
When I'm with my Lord.*

Praying During Severe Trials and Temptations

All of us must pass through trials and temptations sometimes lasting for days or weeks. There are times when we are tempted to doubt God. Doubts concerning our faith torment us. We begin to doubt whether God said or meant a certain thing. We doubt whether we are on the right track. We doubt whether God really is alive, whether He is love. At such times I have often found it helpful to repeat Bible verses as pledges from the Lord: "He guides me in the right paths, as he has promised" (Psalm 23:3 GNB). "The Father himself loves you" (John 16:27). "Defeat does not come to those who trust in you" (Psalm 25:3 GNB).

Everything that comes into our lives, every path we have to follow, has been planned by God. If we have made a decision to go a certain way after asking Him in prayer to lead us the right way, we can trust in His guidance. If, later, doubts and misgivings seek to plague us, we can assert: "God is a Father. If His child has asked

---

*Taken from *My Father, I Trust You: Songs of Trust and Dedication.*

Him to lead him along the right way, He cannot lead him along the wrong way. A good father on earth would not do that, and much less our Father in heaven. So I must be going the right way."

If we think that we understand God differently now than we did when we had made the decision, then we can come to Him anew and lay the question before Him. And He will answer us. He will answer either by giving us an inner assurance or through others with whom we discuss the matter, if we ask Him to guide them in what they say. Sometimes God's answer lies in a Scripture verse received in prayer. Our decision about which way to go needs to be confirmed several times — through the Word of God, through other people, through an inner certainty or by other means.

Most important of all, we need to be firmly convinced of the wisdom of God's leadings and refuse to entertain even the slightest doubt. How can He lead us the wrong way if we have asked Him to lead us the right way? If, however, we have good reason to fear that our self-will is still so strong that we cannot differentiate between God's will and our own, we can ask Him to let us recognize our self-will. And God will answer that prayer.

Often we are in inner conflict and wonder whether we are on the right track simply because we find a particular leading too hard. This I know from my own life. And the Scriptures also bear witness to this fact. Every time we run into difficulties, Satan comes and tempts us and tries to lure us away from the path we are treading. That happened to Jesus as He spent forty days in the wilderness in solitude without anything to eat. Satan can get at us when there is something in our circumstances or in God's leading we find hard to bear. Now is his opportunity. Rebellion, even if we are unconscious of it, leads to the reaction: "Perhaps this really isn't the right way for me." These doubts begin to torment us. The more we look at the difficulties with fear, the worse the inner conflict becomes.

In such times of inner conflict it is important to repeat what Jesus said in His hour of temptation in Gethsemane: "Shall I not drink the cup which the Father has given me?" — " My Father . . . not as I will, but as thou wilt" (John 18:11; Matthew 26:39). I have found that the doubts vanish like soap bubbles whenever I say Yes to the path that is so hard for me and accept it unconditionally. I have also found that it is possible for me — indeed, even easy for me — to say Yes whenever I think of the heart of God the Father, which is nothing but love. He does not lead us along difficult paths without refreshing us inwardly. He never lets us be tempted beyond our strength. And for every difficult way He has prepared a glorious end (James 5:11).

Great power lies in saying "Yes, Father." Say Yes and the temptation yields! I have found that abundant blessing lies in such Yes-Father prayers, in the surrender of our will to His. This surrender of will brings us very close to the Lord. Out of union with God new fruit will be produced again and again.

Such prayer in time of inner conflict is of special importance and value. God only leads us into times of testing in order to hear us say Yes. This is more precious to Him than a thousand other prayers, because it is backed by our whole life, yes, often our greatest sacrifice. He repays such prayer more than any other. He answers it with overflowing blessing and a fullness of grace as He seldom would otherwise grant.

Praying Against Sin in Our Lives

Sin is poison. It poisons not only the whole body but also the soul and spirit. It makes us leprous, as it were. It is like spreading cancer. That is why the Lord uses the sharpest expressions when He speaks about our sin. He challenges us to use the sharpest weapons to fight it, to destroy it no matter what the cost. Jesus tells us that we have to hate sin. We must hate our ego with all its demands (Luke 14:26), our self-love, the source of so much sinning. Whenever our sin and bondage are revealed, we should prefer to "pluck out" our eye according to the words of

Jesus, rather than become children of hell (Matthew 5:29). Sin is the poison of hell. Sin comes from Satan. Sin brings people into the hellish regions of death for eternity; that is why praying against sin in our lives means engaging in spiritual warfare.

Just as in the battle for bound souls, it is a matter of fighting against the greatest enemy, Satan himself. He is the one who incites us to sin. He is the one who does not want to allow the bonds to be broken with which he has bound us to himself.

His main tactic is therefore to make us blind so that we cannot recognize our sin. The greatest obstacle in battling against our sin is our self-righteousness. Accordingly, the first step is to ask the Lord to send us His Spirit of truth. By nature we are reluctant to see what we are really like or we try to minimize our sin, but if we are willing, He will give us light. He will show us how loathsome our sin is.

If we persistently beseech the Lord, "Set my secret sins in Your light", if we cry for the spirit of repentance, if we are, above all, willing to accept that which God has others tell us, then we will experience astonishing things. All of a sudden, it will seem as though a curtain has been drawn away. We will recognize the abyss of our ego, the cancerous damage of our disease of sin.

Being wholesomely alarmed about our sin and daily experiencing new defeats, we will then be determined to take up the battle against sin. I have found that it is not enough to tell the Lord every day what my sins are and where I am in bondage and to ask Him to grant me release. No, here it is a matter of proclaiming the victorious name of Jesus over the enemy's might and of claiming the power of His redeeming blood — and not just once. Since such a prayer is a real battle, we need to devote a substantial amount of time to this spiritual warfare.

How do we go about this in practice? When I finally came to the point where I loathed the very thought of my sin and could sense something of what Jesus meant when He said we should take drastic measures against sin in our lives, I made the decision to fight against the power of sin in my life and character, no matter what the cost. Thereupon, I began a real battle. That meant sacrificing twenty minutes of sleep either in the morning or the evening in order to fight against the particular sins that had become unbearable for me. As a help I made a compilation of victory songs, Easter songs and litanies, which I held up against the enemy.

Time and again I began to praise, to sing, to thank God that Satan and the power of sin have been crushed, because Jesus has conquered them on the cross. As the risen Lord He triumphs over death and hell. Over and over again I praised the power of the blood of the Lamb, which redeems us and cleanses us from all sin.

But I also discovered that the enemy does not let go of us easily and how contaminated we are with sin. We are in bondage to it with every fibre of our being. Often, it does not yield so quickly because it goes back for generations in our family. Anger, bitterness, resentment, inability to forgive — how deeply they can be rooted in us! Such feelings and thoughts come over us again and again. Or we find ourselves doing things we don't want to — and all because our sinful passions and drives are too strong for us to resist. Or we may lash out repeatedly in defiance against God or against what others say, arrange or do. Or a judgmental spirit takes us captive. Looking down upon others, we condemn them, thus sinning against the sixth commandment (cf. Matthew 5:21,22).

Powers and principalities are at work here. We cannot expect to be freed in a few weeks or a few months. Even if God does release us suddenly from a particular bondage, we usually need to fight the battle of prayer and faith for a long time against our personality sins, which are so engrained in us.

Not only that, we need to be willing to suffer for our sins. In prayer we need to commit ourselves to the Lord for His disciplinary measures. He showed me that the battle against my sin was not only a matter of battling in faith but also of being surrendered to Him. We have to be willing to follow paths of chastening on which the Lord wants to purify us from our sinful traits. The proud will become humble only when God leads them along paths of humiliation and breaks their pride. For those who cannot forgive and easily become embittered, it may be a wholesome experience of God's chastening to find that others feel unable to forgive them, that others write them off or become bitter towards them.

On such paths of chastening the Yes-Father prayer is again appropriate — this time as we humble ourselves in prayer beneath the mighty hand of God, knowing that we need chastening in order to be released from our sin (Hebrews 12:10). The Bible illustrates this in the life of Jacob. It was not enough to be at the mercy of Laban's cunning and to be tricked into serving him an additional seven years — in return for his own underhandedness and duplicity. Before Jacob could return to Canaan, the land of his inheritance, it was necessary for him to be broken by the struggle at Jabbok. The same thing is demonstrated in the story of Joseph's brothers. They sold him and delivered him up to fear and distress. Later when they came to Egypt to buy grain, they underwent immeasurable fear and distress themselves due to Joseph's acting. For his part, Joseph had to suffer for his vanity, self-glory and pride by becoming a slave and a prisoner.

When we have to suffer painfully for our sins it is important to pray the prayer of the good thief on the cross: "We are receiving the due reward of our deeds" (Luke 23:41), which is very similar to what the brothers of Joseph said (Genesis 42:21). We need to humble ourselves beneath the mighty hand of God. He will hear this prayer together with our prayer of faith. We will be delivered from our sins as truly as Jesus is a Redeemer and as truly as He has accomplished His victory at Calvary for each one of us.

Praying in Times of Need

We all have to go through times of need. For instance, we recall the wartime and post-war periods when there was a shortage of food. We may lack money to buy things essential to our well-being or that of our families. Perhaps financially we are not in a position to care for our children properly or to provide them with the necessary education. Or maybe a family member is sick and we cannot give him the help he needs, because we simply do not have the means.

We can also suffer want in other areas of our lives. We may not have the strength we need to do our job. Or we may lack the necessary co-workers or colleagues. Perhaps we are always pressed for time and find it hard to fit everything into our schedule. What type of prayer can remedy such situations?

First, it is important to make certain whether we are really faced with a situation of need or whether we want to pray away something God has ordained for our lives. With respect to our goods and possessions the Bible says, "If we have food and clothing, with these we shall be content" (1 Timothy 6:8). For instance, there may be something we can't really afford but covet so as to raise our standard of living. If this is so, our prayers will lack the promise of being answered. The same rule of thumb applies to other situations of need. Perhaps in wilfulness or selfish ambition we want to attain something that is not in God's plan for us. Therefore, the first thing is to pray that God will give us His light and His standards. He will show us what we really need and what we should pray for. This is especially important when it concerns something we think is urgently needed for the Lord's work.

I have experienced many genuine times of need in the Sisterhood of Mary and also previously. They have become especially precious to me, because they introduced me to a new type of prayer. This prayer contains incomparable blessings. It is the childlike prayer to God the Father. Periods of want make us dependent upon the Father. That is why they have enriched my spiritual life immeasurably. In dependence upon the heavenly Father we get to know Him, and I have come to know Him as a true Father. I have experienced the truth of the Scripture, "Your Father knows what you need" (Matthew 6:8). He is concerned about the smallest detail.

"Even the hairs of your head have all been counted" (Matthew 10:30 GNB). I can testify to the fact that He rejoices to do good things for us. He rejoices to take good care of His children and to pour out His benefits upon them. He is filled with joy when He sees His children happy and thankful.

Therefore, in times of want come to the Father as His child and say, "My Father, You know what I need. My Father, all things are Yours and You provide all things. My Father, You will not let me suffer want any longer, because Your child has a share in Your wealth. My Father, You will glorify Yourself now in my need. You will reveal Your nature — almighty and full of loving-kindness."

For many years now in the Sisterhood of Mary we have been trusting God to supply our needs. Instead of asking people for help, we have brought our childlike prayers to our heavenly Father. And He has never disappointed us. He gives His children far more abundantly than they ever ask or expect — provided they seek first His kingdom and His righteousness, as it says in His Word. We are not to covet material goods, but rather we are to work and spend ourselves for His kingdom, giving our all to this end. This may also include the willingness to give others what they request, even if we do not have enough. Of course, we must be mindful that our relationship with God and with our fellow-men is in order. Then everything we

need for our daily lives will be ours as well —
according to His promise.

As children of God we may approach Him
with thanksgiving, because He has already
opened His hands for us. Indeed, He never
leaves a prayer of His child unanswered if it is for
something we really need and if we have
removed all the prayer hindrances.

Praying When Burdened with Cares

At times we all have mountains of cares, but we
know that we can move these mountains
through prayer. There are cares which we are
incapable of tearing out of our hearts, cares
which bog us down so that we forget what it is to
be happy. Prayer can help us. Prayer can make
these cares vanish. But what kind of prayer is
necessary?

The cares burdening us can take many different forms. They may concern our personal lives,
our families or others outside the family circle.
Or they may concern our nation, the future, our
career and many other areas of life. Being
responsible for our Sisterhood, I have often
found that these cares and worries descended
upon me like an avalanche. They threatened to
bury me alive. Very often I could not see any
way out. There did not seem to be any feasible
solution.

But then I began to pray certain short prayers in which great power lies: "My Father, I don't know how You are going to help, but one thing I do know — You *will* help." Or "My troubles can never be greater than my Helper. You always have a solution — ways and means are never lacking. I thank You that You, O God, are greater than my troubles." — "I thank You, O God, that You are a God who performs miracles and that I may count on Your miraculous intervention. Mountains melt like wax before You. I thank You that You can move these mountains of cares and cast them into the sea. A single word from You can change everything and solve all my problems."

What happened when I prayed such prayers? Every time I expressed my thankfulness for what God was going to do, every time I thanked Him for His help, it seemed as though my worries were driven away with great force. They retreated. These feelings of worry and anxiety are fed by demonic powers, which are bent on getting us down. They want us to lose heart and to despair. The enemy does his best to make us unhappy, but God does His utmost to make His children happy, because He loves them.

In my experience it is a matter of not giving cares and worries any room. Shut the door! Don't let them in! Losing oneself in cares and worries is trespassing on forbidden territory. They spin a web around us so that we find ourselves in real distress and a state of hopelessness. It is all a device of the enemy, who paints everything black, as though there were no almighty God, as though the cross that is laid upon us were too heavy . . . In these cases we should immediately dismiss such thoughts, renounce them, and begin to think the thoughts of God. That means, we have to think, pray, sing and proclaim who God is. He is the Father of love. He cares for us. We can cast all our anxieties upon Him (1 Peter 5:7).

In the midst of your cares look up to God. Repeat aloud or sing sentences like these: "You are love. You are a Father, and so You will not let me drown in my cares and worries. You are a Helper in the day of trouble. You always know what to do. You are almighty. For You, my problems are never too difficult. You always have a solution, even if I do not see any. You never lay too many burdens upon me. You let all things work for the best for me."

When you have no idea how you will complete your day's work, praise God by saying, "You have planned this day including everything that needs to be done. So it will all work out time-wise." Leave it up to Him to show you how to finish everything. He will see to it that there is enough time. Be joyful, and set about your work.

In this manner bring all your cares and troubles to the Father. When you surrender yourself to Him in childlike trust and leave to Him everything that is weighing heavily upon you, He will take over the responsibility each time.

An important point is that you begin to thank Him for His aid on past occasions when there seemed to be no way out, no solution. This will strengthen your faith for the current situations and all the impossibilities you face. You need to banish cares and worries with prayers of thanksgiving. The prayer of thanksgiving has the power to make these cares yield, and at the same time it is a joy for our Father in heaven.

Praying When Feeling Despondent

We are all acquainted with periods of despondency. Sometimes we think we are a hopeless case spiritually. In spite of all our battles and efforts, the chains of sin seem to bind us tighter than ever. At other times we become discouraged, because we do not have any physical strength or because we are sick and feeling poorly. Or we may be on the verge of giving up, because we feel incompetent for our job and unable to do what is expected of us.

We also know the despondency that comes over us when we seem to be getting nowhere in a task we want to accomplish, or when we lack authority over our children. We despair when we have no influence on them or on others for whom we are responsible. Finally, we come to the conclusion, "I can't do it. It's useless. I'm inadequate. I lack the potential, strength and ability."

Defiance and rebellion against God is the next step. It is actually present in despondency, though usually we are not conscious of this. Ultimately we are accusing Him of giving us such an unfortunate personality, of putting us into these difficult circumstances, of withholding a talent from us or of failing to give us the strength we need, and so on.

Despondency not only makes us unhappy, but it always induces us to sin. That is why we need to pray for release from our despondency. In my experience the way to victory consists firstly of the prayer of acceptance. We need to say Yes to the fact that we are sinners, to our spiritual poverty, our inabilities and weakness. Since this has been laid upon us by God, we need to accept it. He only gives us the very best, because in His love He has planned every area of our lives — including our weakness and inability. Again, it is His love which allows us to suffer for our bondage. Through this breaking process He wants to strengthen the new man in us. Therefore, the best thing that could happen to us is to be poor in some respect or other.

This was also the experience of the apostle Paul. He too was not delivered from his "thorn in the flesh", which may have been an eye disease, although he desperately needed his sight for his ministry. However, God did not take this affliction from him. First, God wanted to have his dedication, his Yes. The acceptance of his "thorn in the flesh" was more important to God for Paul's ministry than his health. Such a surrender of the will, backed by a great sacrifice, was the "salt" that would empower his ministry. What dynamic power lies in every Yes-Father prayer!

God will never accept an act of dedication without giving something in return. Holy Scripture tells us this time and again. Whoever makes a sacrifice, whoever loses his life, is to receive a hundredfold — good measure, pressed down, shaken together, running over. So when we surrender ourselves in prayer and say Yes to our poverty and inability, to our weakness and humiliation, we will find that our Father has prepared a special present for us in His love.

God promised the apostle Paul that He would demonstrate His power all the more in his weakness. And we may claim this promise for ourselves too. So when we are feeling despondent, we should not only pray a prayer of dedication, but also pray something along these lines: "I thank You that I may await Your help. You see my helplessness in the face of my bondage, and You want to reveal the power of Your redemption and glorify Yourself. And in my inadequacy and lack of talent for my job, You want to assist me and provide for me from Your abundant wisdom, so that the work can be accomplished much better than if I had had the best natural abilities, for what is achieved will come from You and not from me."

There is always blessing, authority, victory and matchless glory in that which comes from God. We receive a much greater blessing than if we had achieved something with our own natural abilities.

So let us follow the example of the apostle Paul and say, "I will boast of my weakness. I will rejoice in my weakness, my inability, my poverty in some particular area in my life. I will rejoice that I am poor in my own righteousness, in strength, in beauty, in talents, in popularity." Start thanking the Lord, for now you will begin to experience His glory, which He will demonstrate in your poverty and inability.

Then all of a sudden you will become happy and you will rejoice that the Lord let you become poor in a certain respect, not giving you this or that. Why? — Because the Lord wanted to give you something precious, something of eternal value. It will radiate from you to others. By this they will be much more blessed than if you had been naturally gifted.

A person with a difficult personality may have many struggles. If, however, as a result of these struggles, he enters into a deeper relationship with Jesus and through His forgiveness experiences transformation in character, he will radiate the image of Jesus much more than a person who is naturally harmonious and good, who can rely upon his own resources. Similarly, if a person with ugly, unattractive features is aglow with the Spirit, he will be more radiant and a greater blessing to others than a person who is naturally beautiful, but living without God. The latter cannot bless others. At the most he could stimulate them to sin.

If a mother lacks the ability to bring up her children, she is driven to call upon the help of God hour after hour and ask Him to give her the right words. From God Himself she will receive ideas and words which will benefit her children far more than any inborn talents.

Times of despondency should compel us to pray more than ever, for only through prayer will we be lifted out of our despondency. We need to accept the fact that we are weak, and we should praise God for His desire to glorify Himself through our weakness. Times of despondency, when we suffer because of our inability, will yield a special blessing for us if we practise this kind of prayer.

Praying When Afraid

Fear! How can we conquer it? How can prayer help us? When fear fills the heart, it burns us out like fire. We can hardly find words to pray. It takes complete control over us!

Fear! We know what it is like when fear descends. It is paralyzing. We are no longer capable of taking the next step. We act as though we had been hypnotized. We can hardly move.

Fear! We know what suffering it causes us. It robs us of every joy, of every hope, of every assurance.

Fear is the affliction that torments most people nowadays — even if they do not want to admit it. Jesus' prophecy for the last days is beginning to be fulfilled: "Men fainting with fear and with foreboding of what is coming on the world" (Luke 21:26). This has already begun to happen to people, especially to those who are alert and are observing world events with open eyes.

Is there any type of prayer which could possibly help us when our hearts are full of fear?

Yes, there is! I can testify to it, because I am by nature a fearful person. During the war I was afraid of air raids. In times of danger I was afraid of evil persons and attacks. And by nature I am afraid of the horrors of a coming nuclear war. However, I have really experienced that Jesus is greater and stronger than my fear. Through prayer we can master fear instead of it mastering us.

We banish fear through the name of Jesus Christ. Jesus in His love understood us when He said, "In the world you have tribulation" (John 16:33). But then He went on to say that we should be of good cheer, because He has overcome the world. And He meant that He has overcome the world with all its fear and tribulation. He has conquered it and laid it at His feet. And He has promised us, "My peace I give to you" (John 14:27). Every promise is a cheque which He will honour whenever we remind Him of it and lay it before Him on the counter. A time will come when we need what He has promised and when that time comes, He will make good His word.

However, one point is important. We do not constantly have the same degree of fear in our hearts. During the times when fear is not throttling us, we need to pray a great deal and continually hold up the promise of Jesus: "You want to impart Your peace to my heart. Fill my heart now with Your peace so that fear will find no room when it seeks to enter."

Now is the time to pray that Jesus will fill our hearts with peace — before the time comes when we actually have to suffer the horrors of a nuclear war or are exposed to a severe persecution as Christians. Now, when faced with lesser agitations, problems and worries, let us practise abiding in peace. This is our opportunity to try it out. Whenever we have any problems and troubles, we can call upon the name of Jesus and claim in faith His pledge to us: "My peace I give to you."

Let us learn now to keep on claiming the promise of Jesus in faith: "I have overcome the world." Yes, He overcame the world for us. The horrors of this world need not dominate our lives. We may count on Him being with us, He who has redeemed us, so that fear and distress cannot get the better of us.

It is also a matter of committing ourselves through Jesus to the Father in complete trust. The most powerful and most beneficent Father is our shield and our fortress, a stronghold in the day of trouble. He knows those who trust in Him.

If we practise praying in this manner now whenever lesser fears and cares arise, then one thing is certain: when greater fears come into our lives — in the coming times we will all, more or less, experience fear — then we will be like an equipped warrior, a skilful fighter, who knows how to defeat this enemy called fear.

Let us make the most of our time. Today we need to tackle this problem of fear. Today we need to gain the victory over our lesser fears. When we have experienced how Jesus comes to us in our minor worries and troubles and fills our hearts with His peace, then we will have far more courage and faith and a deeper assurance that He will do the same for us when we are faced with deeper fears.

Jesus is greater than everything, greater than the most profound fear that can befall us. He has put all things under His feet. And He has freed us from all sins and difficulties that seek to oppress us.

Prayer offers us a way out of our fear. It is all a matter of calling upon Jesus' name. Only in

His name is there help. The more we call upon His name, the more we will experience this truth.

Praying for Others

If we truly pray for our own needs, we will naturally pray for those of others too — whether they are family or church members or other people whom God has brought into our lives. Perhaps we do this day by day. We hold them up before Jesus, asking Him to convert, guide, bless them or free them from a particular sin. All this is good. It is important that we bless those for whom we pray.

However, over the years the Lord has shown me more and more clearly how important it is, when wrestling for the salvation of a soul, not to overlook a certain power. That power is Satan. He keeps a tight hold on souls. He has but one purpose — to prevent them from becoming the trophies of Jesus Christ. He does everything possible to prevent a person from repenting. He does not want people to be freed from their sins, be transformed in character and become happy.

If we just ask Jesus to be with a certain person and help him to become free, and that this person may be born again through the Spirit of God, then we neglect the fact that Satan still has him in his grip. Our prayers miss the mark; they do not deal with the real cause of the problem. An increasing number of people today — including many believers — have become slaves of Satan through occultism or bondage to some sin. They can only be set free when we pray with authority, forcing Satan to yield his prey. We need to use the weapons which are at our disposal for this battle.

For example, we need to call upon the blood of the Lamb. First, we must claim His blood for ourselves when we begin to wrestle in prayer for other souls, so that Satan does not have the slightest right to us and so that our prayers are granted authority. Second, we are daily to lay the blood of the Lamb upon the bound soul and to pray and sing, for instance, "The blood of the Lamb will redeem you and set you completely free." The Lord has shown me how important this is. There is great power in the blood of the Lamb. Satan cannot bear to hear someone call upon the blood of Jesus, with which He redeemed us: he is forced to release souls.

Intercessory prayer has taught me something else: the power in the name of Jesus. When we proclaim the victorious name of Jesus, strongholds of Satan fall and he has to surrender captive souls. When praying for someone in bondage, we need to proclaim again and again words like the following:

Let praises ring aloud this day,
That Jesus' name has power
To break apart the chains of sin
    that hold . . . captive.

Such prayer has even more power when it is sung. Augustine said, "Singing is threefold praying."

The impact of intercessory prayer is greater still when a number of people come together to proclaim the name of Jesus over a person or group of people in song or spoken prayer. We may find it helpful to use victory litanies praising the name of Jesus and His wounds, which even hell must acknowledge as the token of the ransom price paid for our redemption. The name of a person or group concerned can be inserted in each petition. When people devote themselves to such intercession, their prayers will always result in release for souls in bondage. The effectiveness of intercession depends on how sincere it is. A sign that we take something seriously is that we devote time and energy to it, considering it more urgent than anything else.

We show that our prayer is earnest when we take time every day to pray for certain people or groups of people, and if possible, come together with others for a battle of prayer. Satan's power will always be broken. The Lord alone determines the length of the battle. It depends upon the stubbornness of the case. Sometimes much patience and perseverance is required, but Jesus will always grant victory in response to this prayer.

Praying — A Daily Conversation with God

What should be the content of our daily prayers? In any event our prayers will include the battle of faith against sin, and intercession. But the rest will differ from situation to situation. It will depend upon whether we are in a dry period or in a time when prayer comes easily to us; it will depend upon whether there are certain needs we have to pray about or whether we have to fight against cares or doubts that seek to oppress us.

Yet this is not all. Praying means coming to God the Father and to Jesus with our whole being. We meet with Him. We are aware that He is there, that we are approaching Him, that we are beginning a conversation with God. For what is prayer? Is it anything other than conversation with God? Everyone can enter into such a conversation, for a child has a right to speak with his father and pour out his heart. And so, just as a child can tell his father everything, a child of God can tell his Father and his Lord and Saviour Jesus all that is on his heart. It makes God the Father happy when His child comes to Him with everything. Jesus, our Saviour and Physician, is happy when the sick come to Him with their ailments. And as our heavenly Bridegroom, He rejoices when His bride says loving words to Him.

What grace it is that we sons of men are permitted to speak with God! We can really do as the psalmist invites us to do: pour out our hearts before God (Psalm 62:8). We should pour out everything that moves our hearts — every disappointment, every trial and temptation we cannot conquer, problems with other people, everything that weighs us down. When we tell Jesus everything, we will hear His answers in our hearts. Perhaps He will admonish us or comfort us. Perhaps He will direct our thoughts in a certain way so that we can receive help.

I have discovered that entering into a daily conversation with God is the greatest help. I turn all my problems and all my troubles into a conversation with Him. Not only do my cares vanish, but also I remain continually in contact with Him.

This daily, quiet time of prayer, this daily conversation with God, has brought me a still more precious gift. It reveals to me the Father's loving heart. He waits for His children to express their love to Him in words and dedication. "Draw near to God and he will draw near to you" (James 4:8). Draw near to Him! When we draw near to Him, we should praise Him in word and song by proclaiming who our Father is. He is the kindest Father; He is the most merciful Father; He has a heart filled with love; He is the Father of patience and grace; He is the Father of comfort; He is faithful; His name is Yes and Amen. Then He draws near to us, and we rejoice to know that we are His children and are secure in Him. In this way we draw close to His heart.

Jesus, too, is waiting for us to draw near to Him. Jesus is love. That is why He calls Himself the Bridegroom. He is waiting for the commitment of His bride; He is waiting for her love. We draw near to Him by worshipping and adoring Him. We magnify His name by declaring who He is. He is the Fairest of the sons of men. He is the Lamb upon the highest throne. He is the Well-Spring of joy. He is King of kings, the Prince of victory, who defeated hell and death. Then our love for Him will grow stronger, and He will incline Himself to us. The Scriptures testify to this. "I love those who love me" (Proverbs 8:17), and Jesus promises to make His home with the one who loves Him (John 14:23).

It naturally follows that this daily conversation also brings us into contact with the Holy Spirit. We need His guidance for all our problems and questions, which we pour out before God. It is the Holy Spirit who reveals the glory of the Father and the Son to us. He comes upon us as the Spirit of adoration. Yes, He is always there when we draw near to the heart of God the Father and of Jesus.

Daily prayer should bring us close to the heart of God. Otherwise, it does not fulfil its purpose. It is not sufficient to pray for our needs and the needs of others and to fight the battle of faith against our sins. All this is necessary but not enough. The main point is that our heart draws near to the heart of God. In this union, which is the highest form of prayer, we will make genuine commitments to the Lord. When we worship and adore Jesus, we will be motivated by His love to surrender ourselves to Him more fully and to bring Him sacrifices. Perhaps in such times of prayer we will even commit these acts of dedication to writing. Inspired by the ardour of His love, our daily times of prayer will become a flame of love — nourished by dedication and sacrifice — which will pass on its fire from one day to the next.

This conversation of love with God the Father, with our Lord Jesus Christ and with the Holy Spirit is the crown of all prayer. It is also the root of all genuine prayer. Only what is born of love bears divine life. God is eternal, divine life, because He is love. Only such a life of prayer brings forth fruit without end.

> Always I would think of Thee.
> Jesus, grant me this one plea.
> Take, O Lord, all that is mine.
> Let me be for ever Thine.

Other literature by M. Basilea Schlink

SONGS AND PRAYERS OF VICTORY 84 pages

As Christians we are called to fight the good fight of faith. Yet sometimes it is hard to find the right words. Many have found this selection of songs and prayers to be a great help in praying for themselves or for others.

SONGS FOR SPIRITUAL WARFARE 48 pages

Here we are offered spiritual armament for overthrowing satanic strongholds, freeing captives, cancelling curses and experiencing release from demonic bondage and oppression. In an age when demons and curses are a greater reality than ever, we need to know how to turn Satan's attacks to our advantage.

REPENTANCE — THE JOY-FILLED LIFE 96 pages

"For the past two weeks I felt as if the corners of my mouth had been permanently tied down so I couldn't laugh or smile and I wondered why. Jesus has shown me that I had a few loose ends in my life and some very deep repenting to do. I am so thankful for what He has done because I can smile now and I feel it inside and out."

BRIDE OF JESUS CHRIST 64 pages

No unattainable goal is described here, but the ultimate which the love of God has planned for us. All those who long to draw nearer to Him will find an answer to their quest in these pages.

REALITIES OF FAITH 144 pages

"This is a book for a prayer group, for it is so faith-inspiring. It makes wonderful reading for family devotions; your children will love the stories. Your life will never be the same after you've had a taste of *Realities of Faith*."

Larry Christenson